D1716432

BOOK WORMS

GUESS WHO

Hops

Apple Jordan

mc **Marshall Cavendish**
Benchmark
New York

My fur is soft.

It keeps me warm.

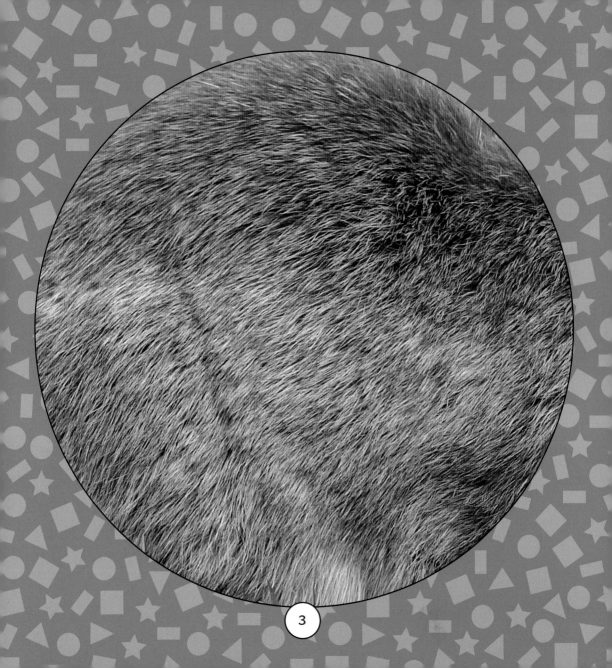

3

My ears are long.

I turn them when I hear a noise.

5

I **twitch** my nose to sniff.

I can smell very well.

My tail is short and fluffy.

My back legs are strong.

They help me hop.

I see danger.

I thump my leg to warn
my friends.

13

I am an **herbivore.**

I eat plants and grass.

I live in a **burrow**.

It is a hole in the ground.

Who am I?

I am a rabbit!

Who Am I?

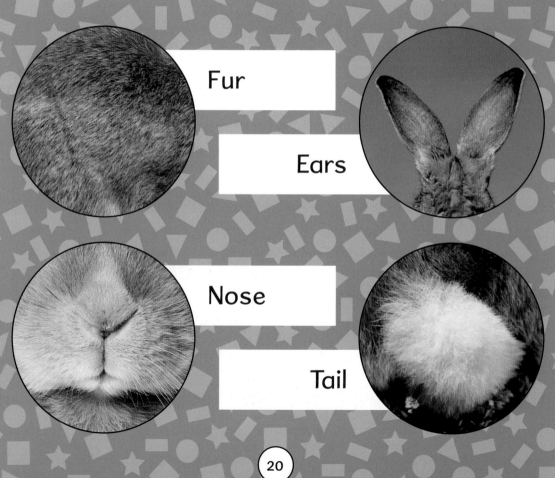

Fur

Ears

Nose

Tail

Legs

Challenge Words

Burrow (BUR-oh) a hole in the ground

Herbivore (HUR-ba-vohr) an animal that eats plants and grass

Twitch (twich) to wiggle

Index

Page numbers in **boldface** are illustrations.

About the Author

Apple Jordan has written many books for children, including a number of titles in the Bookworms series. She lives in upstate New York with her husband and two children.

With thanks to the Reading Consultants:

Nanci Vargas, Ed.D., is an Assistant Professor of Elementary Education at the University of Indianapolis.

Beth Walker Gambro is an Adjunct Professor at the University of St. Francis in Joliet, Illinois.

Other Marshall Cavendish Offices:
Marshall Cavendish International (Asia) Private Limited, 1 New Industrial Road, Singapore 536196 • Marshall Cavendish International (Thailand) Co Ltd. 253 Asoke, 12th Flr, Sukhumvit 21 Road, Klongtoey Nua, Wattana, Bangkok 10110, Thailand • Marshall Cavendish (Malaysia) Sdn Bhd, Times Subang, Lot 46, Subang Hi-Tech Industrial Park, Batu Tiga, 40000 Shah Alam, Selangor Darul Ehsan, Malaysia

Marshall Cavendish is a trademark of Times Publishing Limited

Library of Congress
Cataloging-in-Publication Data

Jordan, Apple.
Guess who hops / Apple Jordan.
p. cm. — (Bookworms: guess who)
Includes index.
Summary: "Following a guessing game format, this book provides young readers with clues about a rabbit's physical characteristics, behaviors, and habitats, challenging readers to identify it"—Provided by publisher.
ISBN 978-1-60870-427-9
1. Rabbits—Juvenile literature. I. Title.
QL737.L32J67 2012
599.32—dc22   2011000332

Editor: Joy Bean
Publisher: Michelle Bisson
Art Director: Anahid Hamparian
Series Designer: Virginia Pope

Photo research by Tracey Engel

Cover: Danita Delimont/Alamy
Title page: Tierfotoagentur/Alamy

The photographs in this book are used by permission and through the courtesy of: *Alamy*: blickwinkel, 3, 20 (top, left); Tierfotoagentur, 9, 20 (bottom, left); Juniors Bildarchiv, 11, 20 (bottom, right); Rolf Nussbaumer Photography, 15; Neil Hunt, 17; Arco Images GmbH, 19. *SuperStock*: Belinda Images, 5, 20 (top, right). *Shutterstock*: Stefan Petru Andronache, 7, 21; Studiotouch, 13.

Printed in Malaysia (T)
1 3 5 6 4 2